COLOR YOUR WAY TO BETTER FOCUS

ART FOR MINDFULNESS
LANDSCAPES

PATTERNS BY JOE BRIGHT

HarperCollins*Publishers*
1 London Bridge Street
London SE1 9GF
www.harpercollins.co.uk

First published by HarperCollins*Publishers* in 2015
1 3 5 7 9 10 8 6 4 2

Patterns by Joe Bright
Introduction text by Imi Lo

Library of Congress Cataloging-in-Publication Data available upon request.

ISBN 978-0-00-794750-8

Printed and bound in China

Introduction

Mindfulness has become extremely popular in recent years, as scientists discover more about the wide array of benefits it has to offer—reducing stress, increasing joy, enhancing emotional intelligence, and undoing bad habits. Although it can be defined in various ways, mindfulness is most simply described as approaching the present moment non-judgmentally, and with curiosity. It offers a break from our incessant, autopilot mind and provides the opportunity to live a fuller life.

Despite urban myth, mindfulness practice is not simply about sitting uncomfortably or chanting "Omm." *Art for Mindfulness* lies in the intersection of mindfulness and therapeutic art, offering a doorway into mindfulness that is accessible, relatable, and fun. Feeling burdened by the chaos of modern life, many adults have found that coloring helps them reconnect with a simpler, more spontaneous way of being.

In order to reap the most benefits from this book, I would invite you to approach it with a playful and curious attitude. A few partially colored-in patterns follow for use as inspiration before you embark on your own work. However, despite what your art teacher may have told you in school, there is absolutely no right or wrong way of coloring. You may be pleasantly surprised by the outcome when you trust your instinct and allow color and strokes to naturally unfold; you may discover a deep sense of calm when you begin to pay the activity your full attention. You may also find this to be a great way to develop more soulful connections with those around you. I hope that you not only enjoy this book, but also discover a deeper layer of spiritual practice through immersing in the art of mindful coloring.

Imi Lo (UKCP, HCPC, MMH), Art Psychotherapist and Mindfulness Teacher

"If opportunity doesn't knock, build a door."

Milton Berle

"Muddy water is best cleared by leaving it alone."

Alan W. Watts

"Mindfulness is the miracle by which we master and restore ourselves."

Thích Nhất Hạnh

"Look at a tree, a flower, a plant. Let your awareness rest upon it. How still they are, how deeply rooted in being. Allow nature to teach you stillness."

Eckhart Tolle

"Look past your thoughts so you may drink the pure nectar of this moment."

Rumi

Be present. Nothing more.

"Some people feel the rain. Others just get wet."

Bob Marley

"To see a world in a grain of sand
and heaven in a wild flower,
hold infinity in the palm of your hand
and eternity in an hour."

William Blake

"There are things known and there are things unknown, and in between are the doors of perception."

Aldous Huxley

"Only when you drink from the river of silence shall you indeed sing."

Kahlil Gibran

"Refuge to the man is the mind; refuge to the mind is mindfulness."

Buddha

"When I let go of what I am, I become what I might be."

Lao-Tzu

"Walking mindfully is having an awareness of your surroundings. It is simpler than you might think."

Rus VanWestervelt

"Do not weep; do not wax indignant. Understand."

Baruch Spinoza

"All know that the drop merges into the ocean. But few know that the ocean merges into the drop."

Kabir

"You must live in the present, launch yourself on every wave, find your eternity in each moment."

Henry David Thoreau

"If we surrendered to earth's intelligence, we could rise up like rooted trees."

Rainer Maria Rilke

"The intuitive mind is a sacred gift, and the rational mind is a faithful servant. We have created a society that honors the servant and has forgotten the gift."

Albert Einstein

**"Every day, think as you wake up:
Today I am fortunate to have
woken up. I am alive. I have
a precious human life.
I am not going to waste it."**

The Dalai Lama

"Remember then: there is only one time that is important—now! It is the most important time because it is the only time when we have any power."

Leo Tolstoy

"Mindfulness is not about getting anywhere else."

Jon Kabat-Zinn

"Learn to get in touch with the silence within yourself and know that everything in this life has a purpose."

Elisabeth Kübler-Ross

**"Be still.
The quieter you become,
the more you can hear."**

Ram Dass

"There is more to life than increasing its speed."

Mahatma Gandhi

**"We need to be willing
to let our intuition guide us,
and then be willing to follow that
guidance directly and fearlessly."**

Shakti Gawain

"The moment one gives close attention to anything, even a blade of grass, it becomes a mysterious, awesome, indescribably magnificent world in itself."

Henry Miller

"The goal of life is to make your heartbeat match the beat of the universe, to match your nature with Nature."

Joseph Campbell

"In the midst of movement and chaos, keep stillness inside of you."

Deepak Chopra

"Silence and spaciousness go together. The immensity of silence is the immensity of a mind in which a center does not exist."

Jiddu Krishnamurti

"The only true voyage would be not to travel through a hundred different lands with the same pair of eyes, but to see the same land through a hundred different pairs of eyes."

Marcel Proust

"Chance is always powerful.
Let your hook be always cast;
in the pool where you least expect it,
there will be a fish."

Ovid

"Forget about enlightenment. Sit down wherever you are and listen to the wind that is singing in your veins."

John Welwood

"We spend precious hours fearing the inevitable. It would be wise to use that time adoring our families, cherishing our friends, and living our lives."

Maya Angelou

"Slowly slowly O mind…
Everything in own pace happens,
Gardner may water a hundred buckets…
Fruit arrives only in its season."

Kabir

"Perfection of character is this: to live each day as if it were your last, without frenzy, without apathy, without pretence."

Marcus Aurelius

"What lies behind us and what lies before us are tiny matters, compared to what lies within us."

Ralph Waldo Emerson

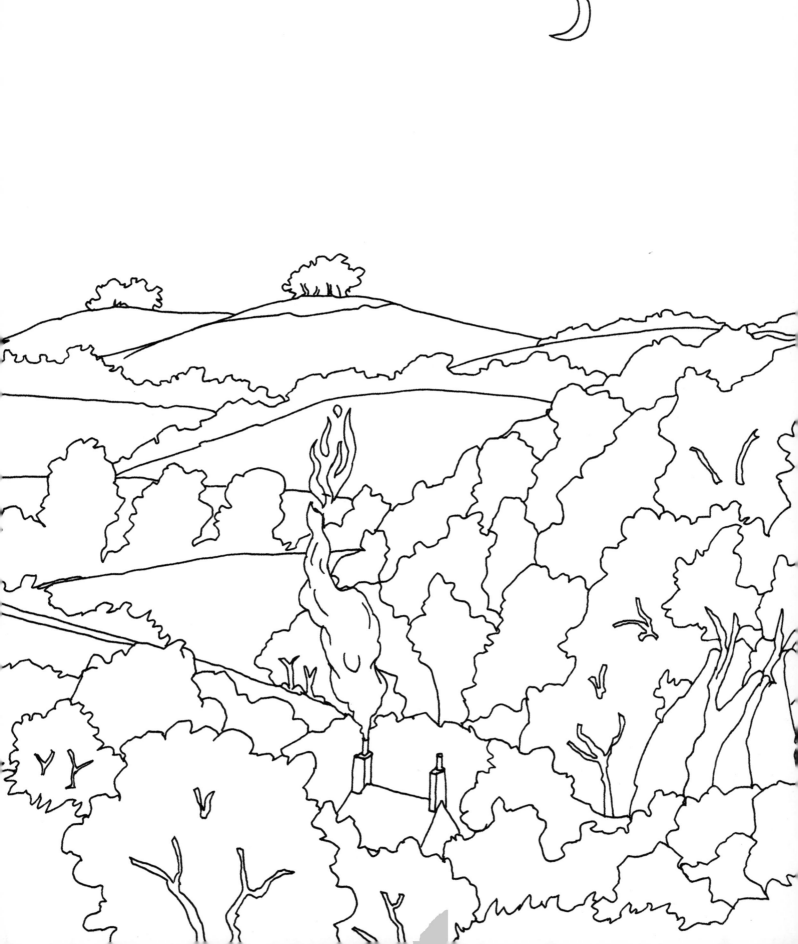

"Slow down and enjoy life. It's not only the scenery you miss by going too fast—you also miss the sense of where you are going and why."

Eddie Cantor

"The noun of self becomes a verb. This flashpoint of creation in the present moment is where work and play merge."

Stephen Nachmanovitch

"Mindfulness isn't difficult; we just need to remember to do it."

Sharon Salzberg

"If you surrender completely to the moments as they pass, you live more richly in those moments."

Anne Morrow Lindbergh

"When we open the invisible doors, we can come to rest in the life we have; we can love it as it is instead of waiting for a shinier version."

John Tarrant

"Do not dwell in the past, do not dream of the future; concentrate the mind on the present moment."

Buddha

"Whatever the present moment contains, accept it as if you had chosen it. Always work with it, not against it."

Eckhart Tolle

"Like an ability or a muscle, hearing our inner wisdom is strengthened by doing it."

Robbie Gass

"Desire, ask, believe, receive."

Stella Terrill Mann

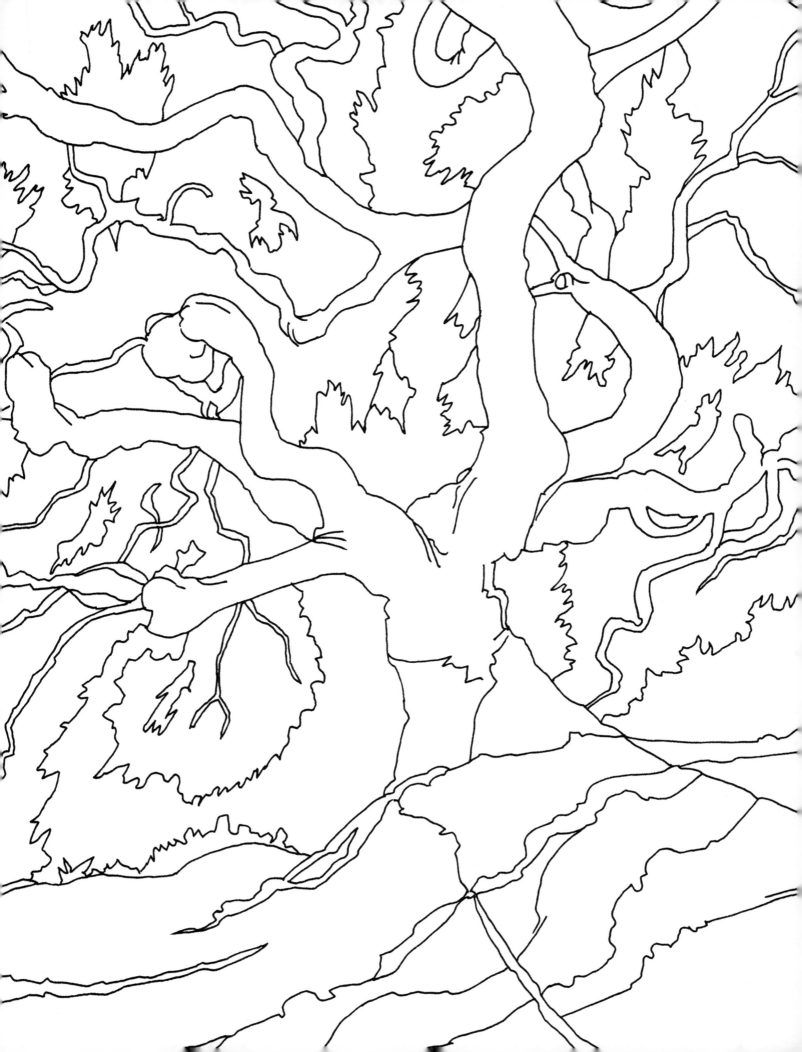

**"Follow your bliss
and the universe will open doors
where there were only walls."**

Joseph Campbell

"He who binds to himself a joy
Doth the winged life destroy;
But he who kisses the joy as it flies
Lives in Eternity's sun rise."

William Blake

"Unless you have been thoroughly drenched in perspiration, you cannot expect to see a palace of pearls on a blade of grass."

Zen koan from *The Blue Cliff Record*

"To be nobody-but-yourself—
in a world which is doing its best,
night and day, to make you
everybody else—means to fight the
hardest battle which any human being
can fight, and never stop fighting."

e. e. cummings

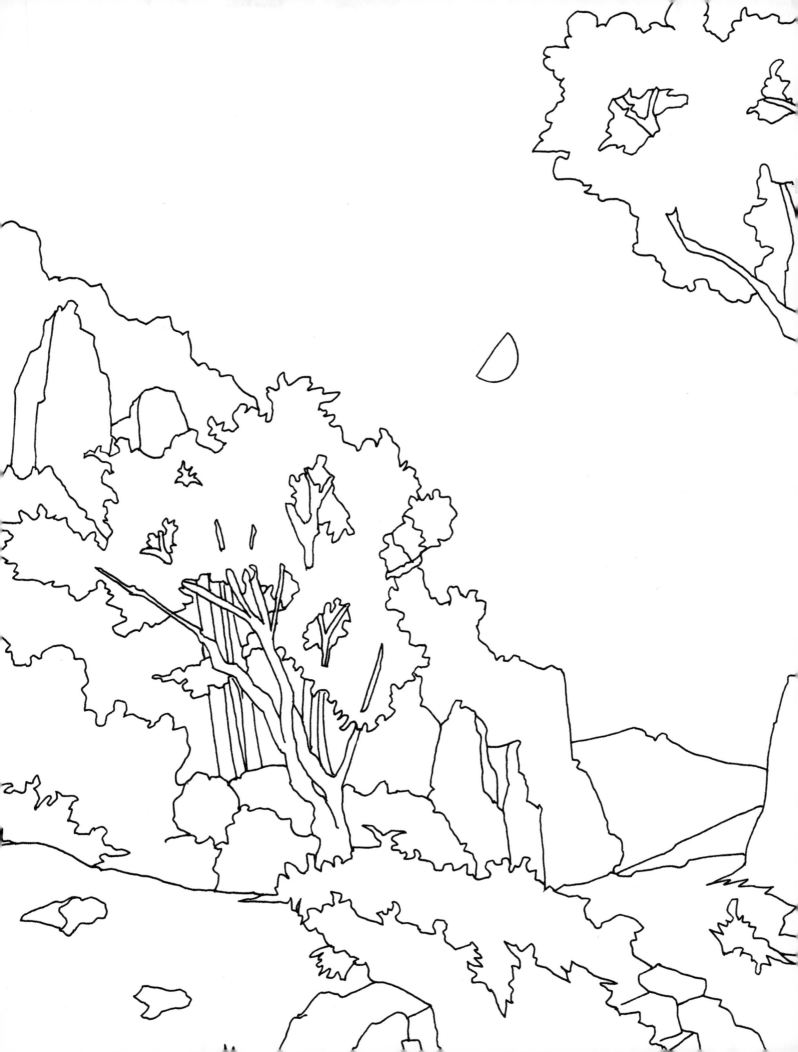

"Nobody cares if you can't dance well. Just get up and dance. Great dancers are not great because of their technique; they are great because of their passion."

Martha Graham

"The mind can go in a thousand directions, but on this beautiful path, I walk in peace. With each step, the wind blows. With each step, a flower blooms."

Thích Nhất Hạnh

"All of you are perfect just as you are...
and there is still room for improvement!"

Shunryu Suzuki

"Silence is sometimes the best answer."

The Dalai Lama

"Out beyond ideas of right-doing and wrong-doing, there is a field. I will meet you there."

Rumi

"If you ask me what I came into this life to do, I will tell you: I came to live out loud."

Émile Zola

"And the day came when
the risk to remain tight in a bud
was more painful than the risk
it took to blossom."

Anaïs Nin

"The art of living…is neither careless drifting nor fearful clinging to the past. It consists in being sensitive to each moment, in regarding it as utterly new and unique, in having the mind open and wholly receptive."

Alan W. Watts

"Life begins at the end of your comfort zone."

Neale Donald Walsch

"Be who you are and say what you feel, because those who mind don't matter and those who matter don't mind."

Dr. Seuss

"Perhaps all the dragons in our lives are princesses who are only waiting to see us act, just once, with beauty and courage."

Rainer Maria Rilke